# Practical Guide to the Operational Use of the Makarov Pistol – 2<sup>nd</sup> Edition

By Erik Lawrence

Copyright ©2014 Erik Lawrence

I0160102

Erik Lawrence
www.vig-sec.com      erik@vig-sec.com

**Printed and bound in the United States of America**

**First printing 2006**
**Second printing 2008**
**Third printing 2014**

**ISBN-10: 1-941998-00-3**
**ISBN-13: 978-1-941998-00-7**
**E-BOOK – ISBN-13: 978-1-941998-20-5**
**LCCN: Not yet assigned**

ATTENTION US MILITARY UNITS, US GOVERNMENT AGENCIES AND PROFESSIONAL ORGANIZATIONS: Quantity discounts are available on bulk purchases of this book. Special books or book excerpts can also be created to fit specific needs. For information, please contact:

Erik Lawrence
www.vig-sec.com      erik@vig-sec.com

CREDITS:
Maxim R. Popenker, Modern Firearms website, http://world.guns.ru

Wikipedia contributors, "Main Page," Wikipedia, The Free Encyclopedia, http://en.wikipedia.org/w/index.php?title=Main_Page&oldid=83971314 (accessed October 7, 2006).

Firearms are potentially dangerous and must be handled responsibly by individuals. The technical information presented in this manual on the use of the Makarov pistol reflects the author's research, beliefs, and experiences. The information in this book is presented for academic study only. Neither the author nor the publisher assumes any responsibility for the use or misuse of information contained in this book.

SAFETY NOTICE
Before starting an inspection, ensure the weapon is cleared. Do not manipulate the trigger until the weapon has been cleared of all ammunition. Inspect the chamber to ensure that it is empty and no ammunition is present. Keep the weapon oriented in a safe direction when loading and handling.

AMMUNITION NOTICE- this weapon fires the 9 x 18mm, not the 9 x 19mm NATO (9mm Luger.)  Firing the incorrect ammunition will damage the weapon and possibly injure the operator.

Training should be received from knowledgeable and experienced operators on this particular weapons system. Vigilant Security Services, LLC provides this training and continually perfects its instruction with up-to-date information from actual use.

www.vig-sec.com

# Table of Contents

**Makarov PM, 9x18mm**

# Section 1

## Introduction

The objective of this manual is to allow the reader to be able to competently use the various Makarov pistols. The manual will give the reader background/specifications of the weapon, instructions on its operation, disassembly and assembly; proper firing procedure; and malfunction/misfire procedures. Operator level maintenance will also be detailed to allow the reader to understand and become competent in the use and maintenance of the Makarov pistol.

## Description

The Makarov PM (Pistolet Makarova), pronounced "muh-KAR-uhv", Russian: *Пистолет Макарова ПМ* is a semi-automatic pistol designed in the late 1940s by Russian firearms designer Nikolai Fyodorovich Makarov. For many years it was the Soviet Union's standard military sidearm.

The Makarov PM is a blowback operated, double action pistol of all-steel construction. The manual safety is located on the left side of the slide, and when engaged, safely brings the hammer down from the cocked position, and then locks the hammer, sear, and slide. The external hammer can be cocked manually for the accurate first shot in single-action mode, or can be cocked automatically by the longer and heavier trigger pull in double-action mode. An all-steel magazine holds eight rounds, and when the last shot is fired, the slide remains in the open position, by to the slide stop. To disengage the slide stop, one must pull the lever on the left side of the frame down. The magazine catch is located at the bottom of the grip. The PM is fitted with fixed open sights as a standard, with click-adjustable open sights available as an option on export models.

The characteristics of the Soviet Makarov pistol:

     A. Country of Origin: USSR
     B. Military Designation: PM (Pistolet Makarova)
     C. Cartridge Type: 9mm x 18mm pistol cartridge
     D. Type of Feed: 8 - round box magazine
     E. Locking System: None
     F. System of Operation: Blowback
     G. Maximum Effective Range: 50 meters

## Background

The Makarov was the result of a competition held to design a replacement for the aging Tokarev TT-33 semi-automatic pistol. The TT had been loosely derived from the popular M1911 and was, by 1945, felt to be too large, heavy, and unreliable for a general service pistol. Rather than building his gun around an existing cartridge, Nikolai Makarov designed a new round, the 9 x 18mm PM, based on the popular Browning 9 x 17mm/.380 ACP cartridge. In the interests of simplicity and economy, the Makarov pistol was to be of straight blowback operation, and the 9 x 18mm round was found to be the most powerful which could be fired safely from such a design. Although the given dimension was 9mm, the bullet was actually 9.3mm in diameter, shorter and wider and therefore incompatible with pistols chambered for the popular 9mm Luger/Parabellum round. This detail meant that Soviet ammunition was unusable in NATO firearms, and in a conflict, NATO forces would not be able to gather ammunition from fallen Soviet soldiers or Soviet supplies.

Makarov called his design the Pistolet Makarova, and it was selected over the competitors because of its simplicity (it had few moving parts), economy, ease of manufacture, accuracy, and reasonable power.

## Design

The Pistolet Makarova (often abbreviated to PM) is a medium-size handgun with a straight blowback action. Physically, it resembles the Walther PPK. As a blowback design, the only thing holding the slide closed is the recoil spring; upon firing, the barrel and slide do not have to "unlock" as with a locked-breech design. Blowback designs are uncomplicated and are more accurate than designs which utilize a recoiling, tilting, or otherwise articulated barrel. Blowback- operated pistols are also limited practically by the required weight of the slide. Conventionally, the 9 x 18mm is the largest round that can practically utilize the blowback operation. The Makarov is relatively heavy for its small size, another desirable attribute for a blowback pistol; a heavy slide provides greater inertial locking against the force of the blast. It also helps absorb a lot of the recoil or "kick" of the 9 x 18mm round.

The Makarov employs a free-floating firing pin and has no firing pin spring. Although this feature allows for the possibility of an accidental discharge if the pistol is dropped from a great height, Makarov felt that the firing pin was of insufficient mass to constitute a major safety hazard.

One notable feature of the Makarov is its extreme simplicity. Many parts perform more than one task: The slide stop is also the ejector. The mainspring powers both the hammer and the trigger, and its lower end serves as the magazine catch. The Makarov has even fewer parts than the Glock, a pistol that was designed with simplicity in mind. Makarov parts seldom break in normal usage, and they are easily replaced with very few tools.

## Operation

The Makarov has a DA/SA or "Double Action/Single Action" operating system. After loading the pistol and charging the slide, one can carry the Makarov with the hammer down and the safety engaged. To fire, the slide-mounted safety is pushed down to the "fire" position, after which the user pulls the trigger. The act of pulling the trigger for the first shot also cocks the hammer, an action which necessitates a long, heavy trigger pull. The firing of the round and cycling of the action precocks the hammer for subsequent shots, which are fired "Single Action" with a short, light trigger pull. After pushing the safety up to "safe," the hammer is safely decocked. Operation is semi-automatic, firing as fast as the user can pull the trigger.

The PM's standard magazine holds eight rounds, although 10- and 12-round capacity magazines were developed later in the Makarov's service life. When the last round in the magazine is fired, the slide locks open. After feeding a new magazine, the user can close the slide by activating a lever (slide stop) on the left side of the frame. This action chambers a fresh round, and the pistol is ready for action again. When engaged, the Makarov's safety prevents the slide from cycling. The Makarov's magazine catch is, as with many European pistols, on the heel or "butt" of the handgrip. This design decision contrasted with the frame-mounted catch of the Tokarev TT-33, as the TT-33's release had a propensity to become snagged on clothing; in the heat of battle, it was easy for soldiers to release the magazine of their pistols accidentally.

## Variants

The Makarov was manufactured in several Eastern Bloc countries during the Cold War and afterwards; apart from Russia itself, they were East Germany, Bulgaria, China, and post-unification Germany, which also found itself with several thousand ex-GDR Makarov pistols.

Countries like Poland and Hungary have developed their own handgun designs that utilize 9x18mm round. Hungary developed PA-63 and Poland has developed the P-64 and the Vanad. While similar in appearance to the PM, being chambered for the same round, and labeled by some US gun retailers as "Makarov," these designs are independent of the PM and have more in common with the Walther PP.

**Figure 1-1 Makarov PM**

## Makarov PM

**Caliber:** 9 x 18mm PM

**Type:** Double action

**Overall length:** 161mm/6.34 inches

**Weight unloaded:** 730g/1.61 pounds

**Barrel length:** 93.5mm/3.68 inches

**Magazine capacity:** 8 rounds

**Figure 1-2 Makarov PMM (Pistolet Makarova Modernova)
Modernized High-Capacity 12 Rounds**

## Makarov PMM

**Caliber:** 9 x 18mm improved (PMM)

**Type:** Double action

**Overall length:** 165mm/6.5 inches

**Weight unloaded:** 760g/1.68 pounds

**Barrel length:** 93.5mm/3.68 inches

**Magazine capacity:** 12 rounds PMM

During the last decades of the 20th century, there were numerous attempts to improve some of deficiencies of the PM, most specifically, its relatively low stopping power and lethality and low magazine capacity. First, an improved version of the cartridge, with lighter bullet and hotter powder charge, was developed as 9 x 18 PMM. This cartridge developed muzzle velocity of 430 meters/1410 feet per second as compared to 315 meters/1033 feet per second of original 9 x 18mm ammo. The large capacity version of the PM was developed along with the new ammo, which included a slight grip frame redesign to accommodate a thicker magazine. Grip panels also were improved. The PMM was offered for both military and law enforcement buyers but did not sell well. Instead, the Russian Army finally went for a new, more promising pistol, developed at the same state-owned Izhevsk Plant.

**Figure 1-3 IJ71H Commercial Export Only Makarov PMM
Modernized High-Capacity 12 Rounds**

## Makarov PMM

**Caliber:** 9 x 17mm (.380 ACP)

**Type:** Double action

**Overall length:** 165mm/6.5 inches

**Weight unloaded:** 760g/1.68 pounds

**Barrel length:** 93.5mm/3.68 inches

**Magazine capacity:** 12 rounds

Export only version of the PPM model.

**Figure 1-4 Makarov PB Suppressed Special Purpose Pistol**

## Makarov PB

**Caliber:** 9 x 18 Makarov

**Type:** Double action

**Weight unloaded:** 970g/2.14 pounds (complete with suppressor)

**Overall length:** 310mm/12.2 inches (complete); 170mm/6.69 inches (with front part of the suppressor removed)

**Barrel length:** 105mm/4.13 inches

**Magazine capacity:** 8 rounds

The PB (*Pistolet Besshumnyj* - Silenced Pistol), also known by the Soviet/Russian army as 6P9, was developed by 1967 for Spetsnaz elements of the Soviet army, as well as for operatives of KGB. The pistol is based on a significantly modified Makarov PM pistol and features a unique integral two-part silencer. The rear part of the silencer is fixed around the barrel, which is drilled to decrease the muzzle velocity to below the speed of sound. The front part of the silencer is quickly detachable, so the pistol can be broken down into two parts for more convenient carry. Unlike many other integrally suppressed pistols the PB can be safely fired with the front part of the suppressor removed, but this option will greatly increase the sound signature. Because the front part of the barrel is enclosed in the suppressor, the slide is made very short and cannot contain the return spring. Instead, the return spring is located in the grip, under the right panel, and linked to the slide via the rocking lever. The double-action firing unit with external hammer and slide-mounted safety/decocker, as well as the magazine, are borrowed from the Makarov PM pistol with no modification. The PB has fixed sights. For carry, it is issued with a special holster that has compartments for the gun and the detached front part of the suppressor.

**Figure 1-5 P-64 Pistol**

## P-64 Vanad

**Caliber:** 9 x 18mm Makarov

**Type:** Double Action

**Weight unloaded:** 635g/1.4 pounds

**Overall length:** 155mm/6.1 inches

**Barrel length:** 85mm/3.35 inches

**Capacity:** 6 rounds

The P-64 pistol (official designation *9 mm pistolet wz. 1964*) was developed in Poland during the late 1950s and early 1960s as a compact and lightweight replacement for Tokarev TT pistols, manufactured in Poland under soviet license. Following the Soviet road, Poland replaced the powerful 7.62 x 25mm ammunition with less powerful, but still effective 9x18 Makarov ammunition. The P-64 has been used by both Polish military and police and can still be found in holsters of some Polish police officers. In military service, it was superseded in the mid-1980s by the P-83 pistol. The P-64 was small and light enough for a pocket or a concealed carry sidearm, but it has too small a magazine and too heavy a trigger pull to be considered as a valuable service pistol. The severely felt recoil also did not help to establish popularity for this gun.

The P-64 is a blowback-operated, semi-automatic pistol made almost entirely of steel. The P-64 is hammer fired, with a double-action trigger and a decocking safety mounted at the left side of the slide. Safety features also include a loaded chamber indicator in the form of a small pin, which protrudes from the back of the slide, above the hammer, when the chamber is loaded with a cartridge. The trigger guard is a separate unit, which is hinged to the frame and serves as a disassembly lever when pulled down. The single-stack magazine contains only 6 rounds, and the magazine catch is located at the bottom of the grip.

# Section 2

## Maintenance

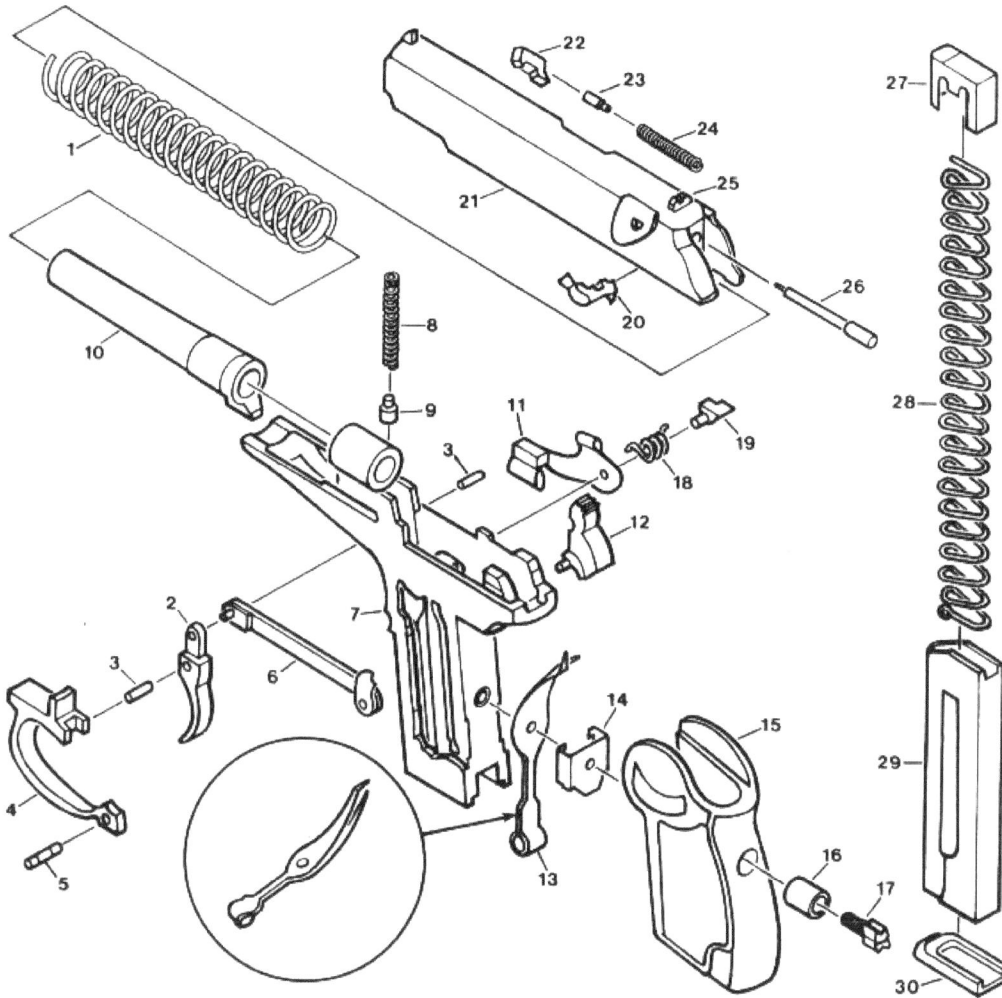

**Figure 2-1 Exploded Diagram of the Makarov Pistol**

| | | |
|---|---|---|
| 1- Driving Spring | 2- Trigger | 3- Trigger Pin |
| 4- Trigger guard | 5- Trigger Guard Pin | 6- Trigger Bar |
| 7- Frame | 8- Trigger Guard Spring | 9- Trigger Guard Spring Plunger |
| 10- Barrel | 11- Slide Stop | 12- Hammer |
| 13- Mainspring | 14- Mainspring Retainer | 15- Grip |
| 16- Grip Screw Bushing | 17- Grip Screw | 18- Sear Spring |
| 19- Sear | 20- Safety Lever | 21- Slide |
| 22- Extractor | 23- Extractor Plunger | 24- Extractor Spring |
| 26- Firing Pin | 27- Follower | 28- Magazine Spring |
| 29- Magazine Body | 30- Magazine Floor plate | |

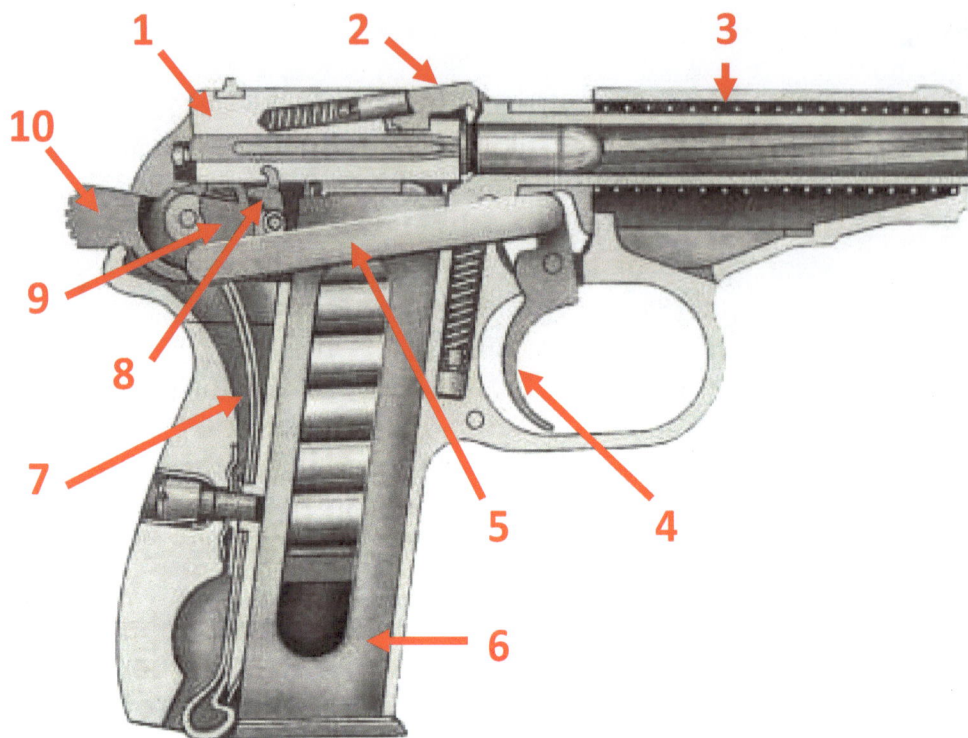

**Figure 2-12 Cross-Section Diagram of the Makarov Pistol**

| | | |
|---|---|---|
| 1- Slide | 2- Ejector | 3- Main Spring |
| 4- Trigger | 5- Trigger Transfer Bar | 6- Magazine |
| 7- Hammer Spring | 8- Sear | 9- Disconnector |
| 10- Hammer | | |

## Clearing the Makarov

**Figure 2-2 Makarov safety in SAFE position**

A. Ensure the pistol is on safe and pointed in a safe direction.

**Figure 2-3a**                    **Figure 2-3b**

B. Remove the magazine by pressing the magazine catch, at the rear bottom of the grip, to the rear (Figure 2-3a) and pull the magazine from the magazine well in the grip (Figure 2-3b). You may have to pull on the front lip of the magazine to free it. Place the magazine in a pocket, magazine pouch or set it down.

**Figure 2-4a**                    **Figure 2-4b**

C. 1- Place the pistol's safety lever on fire and grip the serrations on the slide and 2- pull the slide rearward, allowing the round to extract and eject from the pistol. 3- Press up on the slide stop and release the tension on the slide to lock the slide to the rear Figure 2-4a). Observe the round extracting and ejecting from the ejection port; do not attempt to retain the round.

  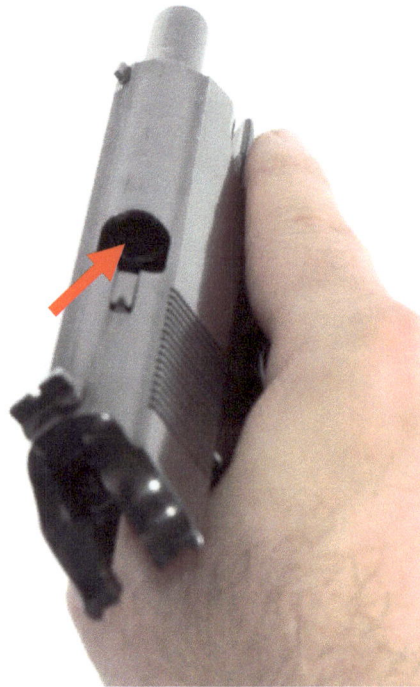

**Figure 2-5a**          **Figure 2-5b**

D. Visually check the chamber for rounds (Figures 2-5a and 2-5b). Once you have ensured the pistol has no magazine in it and the chamber is free of rounds, you now can close the slide by pulling the slide slightly to the rear and riding the slide forward so as not to forcefully shut on an empty chamber.

**Figure 2-6**

E. Place the pistol on SAFE (up position); this will decock the hammer safely (Figure 2-6).

## Disassembling the Makarov pistol

NOTE- Place the pistol's parts on a flat, clean surface with the muzzle oriented in a safe direction.

When the operator begins to disassemble the pistol, it should be done in the following order:

A. Clear the pistol and leave the magazine out and safety off.

B. To remove the slide,

**Figure 2-7 Trigger guard set for disassembly**

1. Pull the front of the trigger guard down.

2. Press the trigger guard to one side when the trigger guard will clear the receiver.

3. Rest the trigger guard against the frame (Figure 2-7).

C. Remove the slide and driving spring.

1. Hold the slide by its milled grooves.

2. Pull the slide fully to the rear of the pistol.

**Figure 2-8 Slide removal step one**

3.  Lift the rear of the slide up and off of the frame (Figure 2-8).

**Figure 2-9 Slide removal step two**

4.  Once the slide is clear of the rear of the frame, ease the slide forward over the barrel (Figure 2-9).

**Figure 2-10 Basic level disassembly**

5.  Pull the driving spring off of the barrel (Figure 2-10). Do not pull from the muzzle end of the spring as this will stretch the spring excessively, slide from the chamber end of the spring where it is attached by its spring tension.

## Reassembling the Makarov pistol

A.  Insure the hammer is cocked, the safety is in the fire position, and the trigger guard is down.

B.  Reassemble and replace the driving spring and slide.

**Figure 2-11**

1.  Slide the driving spring, small end first, over the barrel (Figure 2-11).

**Figure 2-12**

2. Insert the driving spring front end into the circular front section of the slide (Figure 2-12).

3.  Slide the barrel through the hole in the front of the slide.

4.  Pull the slide fully back.

5.  Press the slide down into position on the frame.

6.  The driving spring will drive the slide forward.

7.  Center the trigger guard and rotate it back into the frame.

## Performing a Function Check on the Makarov Pistol

A.   Rotate the safety upward to the safe position (the hammer will fall automatically, but the safety blocks the firing pin).

B.  Press the trigger (the hammer should raise, but not fall).

C.  Rotate the safety downward (fire).

D.  Press the trigger (the hammer should rise and fall).

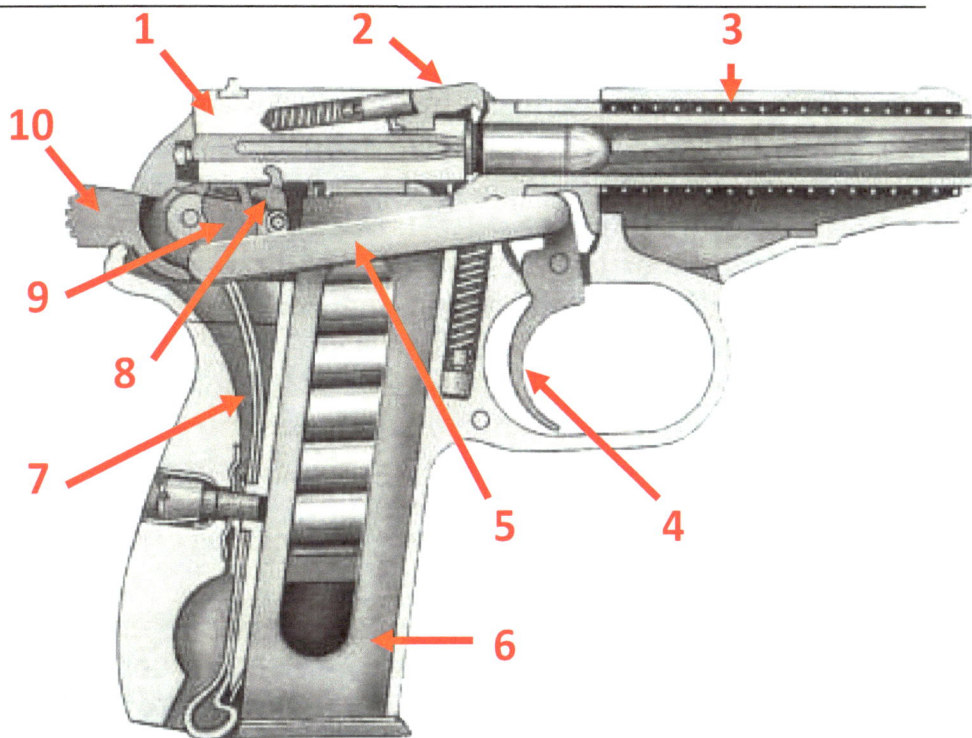

**Figure 2-12 Cross-Section Diagram of the Makarov Pistol**

| | | |
|---|---|---|
| 1- Slide | 2- Ejector | 3- Main Spring |
| 4- Trigger | 5- Trigger Transfer Bar | 6- Magazine |
| 7- Hammer Spring | 8- Sear | 9- Disconnector |
| 10- Hammer | | |

# Section 3

## Operation and Function

### Loading the Makarov Magazine

A. Ensure you have **9 x 18mm Makarov ammunition**; this ammunition is easily confused with 9 x 19mm NATO (9mm Luger) and 9 x 17mm (.380 Automatic). Inspect it for uniformity, cleanliness, and serviceability. Check all cartridges for undented primers and only use issued ammunition.

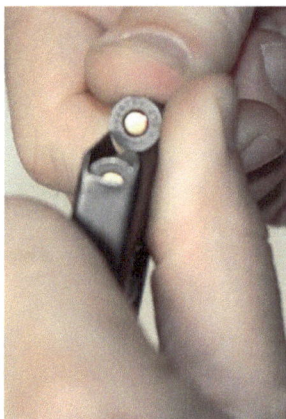 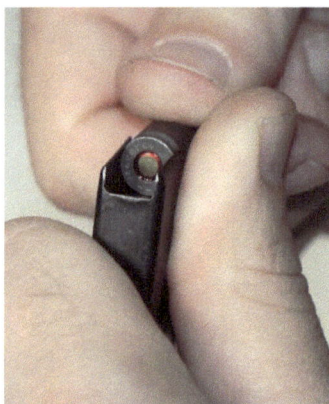 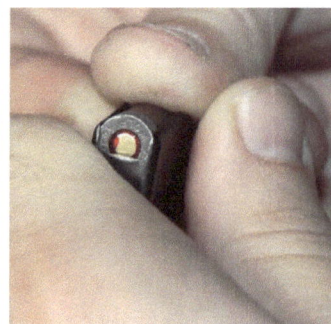

Figure 3-1b        Figure 3-1b        Figure 3-1c

B. Use your non-dominant hand to hold the magazine with the rounded front of the magazine towards your fingertips. Your non-dominant thumb is used as a guide so as not to let the cartridge roll off the follower or other cartridges (Figure 3-1a). With your dominant hand, one at a time, begin with the base of the cartridge at the front of the magazine follower and press the cartridge down and back to insert (Figures 3-1b and 3-1c).

C. The magazine can hold eight cartridges but due to overloading of the spring, do not carry the pistol in this configuration. Load eight and then load the chamber so you have seven in the magazine and one in the chamber. Placing a cartridge in the chamber and releasing the slide stop can cause damage to the extractor, so load the chamber from the magazine only.

## Loading the Makarov Pistol

**Figure 3-2**

A. With the pistol pointed in a safe direction, place the pistol on fire (lower the safety lever).

**Figure 3-3**

B. Lock the slide to the rear by pulling the slide to the rear and pressing up on the slide stop. Once it is engaged, release the slide tension.

**Figure 3-4a**          **Figure 3-4b**

**Figure 3-4c**

C. Insert the loaded magazine into the magazine well (Figures 3-4a and 3-4b). Fully seat the magazine with the heel of the hand to ensure it is locked in by the magazine catch (Figures 3-4c).

**Figure 3-5**

D. Pull the slide by gripping the serrations on the rear of the slide, (not over the ejection port) to the rear and release allowing it to slam shut by its own spring tension (Figure 3-5). To ensure that a round has been chambered either removing the magazine to observe that only seven rounds remain or perform a press check to observe the chambered casing through the ejection port. An alternative method of closing the slide to load is to press down on the slide stop and allow it to shut by its own spring tension. Ensure the slide is in battery (fully forward). Do not close the slide by pressing down on the slide stop unless there are cartridges in the magazine.

**Figure 3-6 Safety in SAFE position**

E.  As the Makarov is a double-action pistol, return the pistol's safety to the safe position to decock the hammer which will in turn decock the hammer (Figure 3-6). The safety blocks the firing pin during this decocking.

## Firing the Makarov Pistol

A.  Orient downrange or towards the threat.

**Figure 3-7 Safety in FIRE position**

B.  Push down on the safety lever to release the safety with a thumb.

**Figure 3-8 Proper firing position**

C. As you orient your sights onto the target, press the trigger straight back so as not to interrupt the sight picture (Figure 3-8). As the Makarov is double action, you will notice your first shot will have a heavier trigger pressure than subsequent shots that are single action (hammer already to the rear). The pistol may also be placed on fire and cock the hammer with your thumb to allow for single-action trigger pressure to fire.

**Figure 3-9 Safety in SAFE position**

D. When you have completed firing the pistol, place the safety lever into the SAFE (up) position (Figure 3-9).

# Section 4

## Performance Problems

### Malfunction and Immediate Action Procedures

Malfunctions are usually preventable through good practices, but they may still occur out of the blue from time to time. Of course, you hope it is on the practice range, but you should treat each one as you are in a life-or-death situation. Practicing proper and effective corrective actions will allow you to be more confident in your pistol handling. In stressful situations, you can become much more stressed due to an unforeseen malfunction that is easy to correct. I have observed many shooters that perceive themselves to be experienced, but when they encounter a stovepipe, they nearly disassemble the pistol rather than sweep it out and continue.

Malfunction drills must fix the problem 100% of the time (excluding a weapon stoppage—broken weapon) the first time performed. You must look at the pistol and identify the problem (obviously the pistol is not functioning as you need so you must transition to another weapon or rectify the situation) it is a non-function weapon at this point—fix it.

You should always practice taking a covered position to correct malfunctions with considerations on how you operate.

The following pages in this chapter describe and detail corrective actions for the various malfunctions that may be encountered.

**NOTE**: The <u>failure-to-go-into-battery malfunction</u>, when your slide does not fully return forward when cycling a round, is always rectified in the same manner, no matter which hand is being used. This malfunction is usually induced when loading and not allowing the full recoil spring tension to shut the slide.

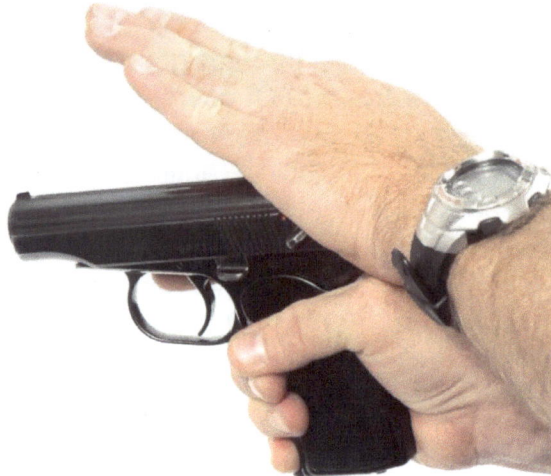

**Figure 4-1 Seating the slide that is out of battery**

To fix a failure-to-go-into-battery malfunction, you must ensure your finger is off the trigger and outside the triggerguard and then slap the back of the slide with the heel of the non-firing hand. If you are shooting while wounded, then you will use your chest or equipment to force the slide forward into battery.

**<u>FAILURE TO FIRE</u>:** This malfunction occurs when the operator has loaded a dud cartridge or failed to load the chamber. The universal fix all for this is the "<u>Slap</u>, <u>Rack</u>, <u>Bang</u>" technique.

**SYMPTOM** - You perform a full presentation to shoot and hear and feel the hammer strike, and the weapon does not fire.

**Figure 4-2 Slap**

**1. SLAP** the bottom of the magazine with a hard palm (fingers extended) to ensure it is fully seated and locked in.

**Figure 4-3 Rack**

2. **RACK** the slide fully to the rear and release it to shut by its own recoil spring tension. You can pivot the slide toward your non-firing hand to assist in racking the slide to the rear; maintain muzzle to threat orientation.

**Figure 4-4 Bang**

3. **BANG** or represent and prepare to fire the shot as you intended before the malfunction if your situation dictates that action.

**FAILURE TO EJECT:** This malfunction (commonly called a "stovepipe") is created usually by the slide being retarded (by not setting one's wrists- "limp wristing") in its rearward movement to rechamber the next round or a broken ejector. This malfunction is easily corrected by sweeping the expended case from the port. The corrective action is the same for vertical and horizontal stovepipes.

**Figure 4-5 Stovepipe**

**SYMPTOM -** You are in the act of shooting a multiple-round engagement, and you notice you cannot see your front sight for a piece of brass is in the way, felt the slide did not fully close, and/or have a soft mushy trigger.

**Figure 4-6a Reach across**     **Figure 4-6b Rearward sweep**

With the non-firing hand, extend your fingers, and with fingers joined, reach over the slide. (DO NOT SWEEP YOUR HAND IN FRONT OF THE MUZZLE.) Roll your fingers over the top of the slide with a firm, vigorous sweeping motion to the rear against the stuck casing to sweep it free (Figures 4-6a and 4-6b). Do not sweep too far as you have to take more time to regrip and present.

**Figure 4-7 Completion of the sweep**

Once the casing is no longer pinched by the slide, the slide will continue to seat the next round, and you are now ready to continue the engagement. Many inexperienced shooters do too much to correct this simple malfunction. **Ensure you do not work the slide fully to the rear when sweeping the empty casing - this action could induce a double feed as the chamber is already loaded**. Continue the engagement as your situation dictates.

**NOTE**:  You must always roll your fingers across so that whichever malfunction you encounter, vertical or horizontal, you will clear it with one sweep.

**Figure 4-8 Present and fire**

**FAILURE TO EXTRACT:** This malfunction (commonly called a "double feed") is created when the spent casing is not extracted from the chamber, and the next round to be loaded is rammed from the magazine into the rear of the stuck casing (Figures 4-9 and 4-10). This malfunction is a serious one since more complicated dexterity is needed to correct it and, of course, to do it quickly. Below is the breakdown of the corrective action to restore your pistol back to operation.

**Figure 4-9 Failure to Extract**

**SYMPTOM -** You are shooting a multiple-shot engagement and notice your slide did not go forward, you have a soft mushy trigger, and it will not fire.

**Figure 4-10 Failure to Extract malfunction**

**Figure 4-11 Step one of corrective action**

**STEP ONE** - With your finger off the trigger, rotate the pistol in your firing hand so you may engage the slide stop with your firing hand thumb. With the non-firing hand, rack the slide to the rear and lock it with the slide stop by pushing it up into the notch, and let the recoil spring tension hold the slide stop in the notch (Figure 4-11).

**Figure 4-12 Step two of corrective action**

**STEP TWO** - Remove the magazine from the pistol (Figure 4-12).

**Figure 4-13 Step three of corrective action**

**<u>STEP THREE</u>** - Rack the slide to the rear at least two times to ensure the casing is extracted and ejected from the pistol. As you are doing this step, observe the casing being ejected and allow the slide to use its force to shut each time it is pulled to the rear. You can rotate the slide towards your non-firing hand to assist in working the slide to the rear.

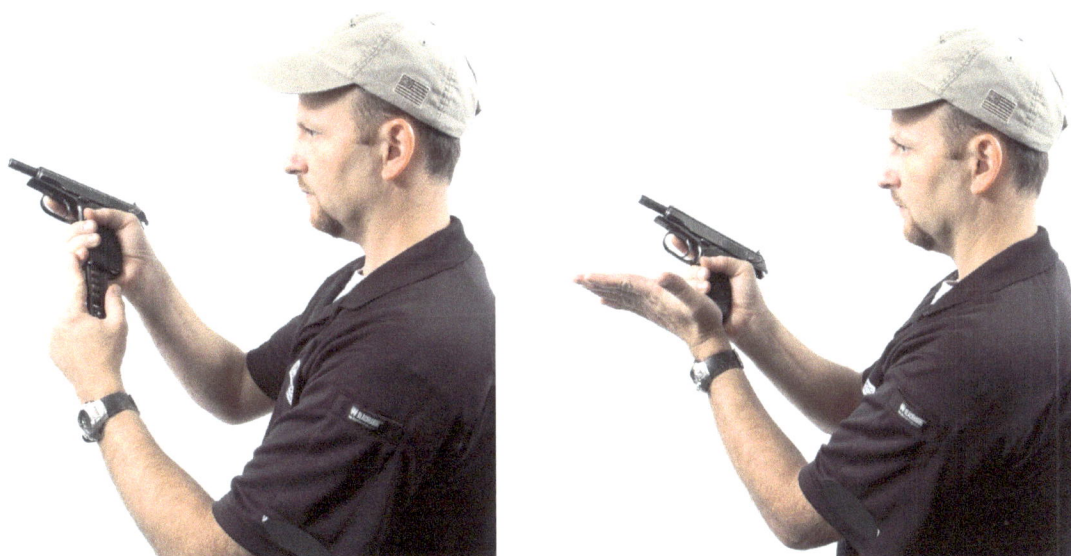

**Figure 4-14 Step four of corrective action**

**<u>STEP FOUR</u>** - Properly insert and seat a loaded magazine with a hard palm (Figure 4-14).

**Figure 4-15 Step five of corrective action**

**STEP FIVE** - Rack the slide fully to the rear and release it to close by its own spring tension (Figure 4-15). Your pistol is now ready to continue the engagement. You can rotate the slide towards your non-firing hand to assist in working the slide to the rear.

**Figure 4-16 Step six of corrective action**

**STEP SIX** - Continue the engagement as the situation dictates (Figure 4-16).

**NOTE**: Correcting this malfunction needs to be practiced often since it is the most complicated to do under stress or when you lose dexterity because blood is leaving the extremities.

## Appendix A - Identification Marking on Makarovs

This appendix was provided from Makarov.com, LLC, 2002, Hurricane, WV.

| East Germany | Soviet Union | Bulgaria |

**A-1 Country Identification Markings**

Countries known to have manufactured Makarov type pistols:
- Soviet Union/Russia – Izhevsk Mechanical Factory
- East Germany – Ernst Thaelmann
- China – Norinco
- Bulgaria – Arsenal
- Germany (post unification) – Simson Suhl

**Russia**

There are several versions of the Russian Makarov. First of all there are the true surplus guns, which are recognizable by their fixed rear sight and a lack of any non-Cyrillic markings including "Made in Russia." Second is the Baikal and Izhmash new production Makarov. These are recognizable by their rear adjustable target sight, "Made in Russia" and Baikal markings. Another variant of this is the 10-round double-stack Makarov, which was also made by Izhmash.

More recently, some of the Russian military Makarovs with fixed rear sights have snuck into the country with shipments of Bulgarian guns. You can usually spot these by the bifurcated triangle with circle marking.

**A-2 IZHMASH Logo**

## How is Izhmash different from Baikal?

IMEZ stands for Izhevskii Mechanicheskii Zavod or Izhevsk Mechanical Factory located in the city of Izhevsk near the Ural Mountains. They produce the Makarov, PSM, various shotguns, air guns, artificial pacemakers for the heart, oil drilling equipment. It is a government, state owned enterprise, but has the right to close its own business contracts and deals without governmental interference.

Baikal is a foreign trade organization this is similar to North China Industries (NORINCO). This was a governmental organization that was used to market Soviet goods abroad. These days Baikal is hardly active in any trade with the US, largely because of the Bill Clinton imposed "voluntary trade restrictions." IMEZ used the grips with Baikal on it because...well, it was all they had.... Baikal also traded autos, trucks, various other consumer goods, not only guns and ammo.

## East Germany

The Ernst Thaelman factory in Suhl, Thueringen made what are considered by some to be the finest pre-fall-of-the-Berlin Wall Makarovs. The finish is nice, the fit and machining is of quality you'd expect from a German shop, and they shoot like a dream. Almost all that came into this country had already seen service, so their quality varies by how they were treated by the person who carried them. Nonetheless, most have more holster wear than bore wear. They occasionally still pop up at dealers and at gun shows.

Note that this **table is not complete** and there appears to be a sequential pattern.

| Production year | Letter Code |
|---|---|
| 1958 | S |
| 1959 | J, K, L, N, U |
| 1960 | B, F, G, H, M, T |
| 1961 | AP*,AR, AS, AQ, AT, AU, AV, AW, AX, AY, AZ |
| 1962 | BR, BT, BU, BV, BW, BX, BY, BZ |
| 1963 | DA, DB, DE, DF, DH, DK, DL, DP, BO, BP |
| 1964 | ES, ET, EV, EX, EZ |
| 1965 | ER, FB, FH, FF |

*\* One person noted that his gun was marked 'AP' and '62,' so there appear to be inconsistencies.*

**A-3 East German production codes** (not a complete list)

## China

Not terribly much is known about these, except that they were brought in as Norinco Model 59. Not many are available, so they often command a premium over other Makarovs. On the whole, the quality of these is not as good as some of the others, but there have been notable exceptions. Very rarely you may run across a Type 59 with an Arsenal mark (number) in a circle. Most common found are 56 and 66. These were Military pistols that were remarked and packed for Commercial Export. A Chinese Makarov with "SHI" mark is of Military issue, and normally if found in the USA means it was a War Trophy "bring Back" from some conflict, and commands a Premium price.

## Bulgaria

The Bulgarian Arsenal Makarovs are the only ones that are currently being imported into the country. Miltex had an exclusivity agreement with Arsenal before they decided to get out of the small arms business. Many other Bulgarian Makarovs are out on the market including some military surplus. As the Bulgarians start to switch to other guns as standard police and military issue, these should continue to pop up everywhere and can be purchased at a very good price. Fortunately for US shooters, these are very nicely done and some interesting variants were delivered by Miltex.

In recent years, the Bulgarians have held the most market share of all the Makarovs. As such, there are variants among these, primarily in grips and markings, including police, military, commercial, and even mis-marked Russians.

## Bulgarian production codes

To find the Year of Manufacture of your Bulgarian "Circle 10" Military Makarov, look at the serial number (S/N), normally found on the left side of the frame, above the grip. The first two letters are the Production series, the next two digits are the Year code, see list below. The last four digits are the unit number in that production series. Please note, the 1970 date is start of all Production at this plant using the "Circle 10" code, the Makarov was first produced under Russian supervision in 1975, and first year of Production under Bulgarian control was 1976.

Some Bulgarian pistols made in 1975 will have the Russian Date format, with the full year in place of the later date codes.

| Year Code | Year Code | Year Code | Year Code |
|---|---|---|---|
| 1970 = 10 | 1971 = 11 | 1972 = 12 | 1973 = 13 |
| 1974 = 14 | 1975 = 15 (Begin Makarov Production under Russian Supervision) | 1976 = 16 (first year Makarov Production, under Bulgarian supervision) | 1977 = 17* |
| 1978 = 18* | 1979 = 19* | 1980 = 20* | 1981 = 21* |
| 1982 = 22 | 1983 = 23 | 1984 = 24 | 1985 = 25 |
| 1986 = 26* | 1987 = 27 | 1988 = 28 | 1989 = 29* |
| 1990 = 30 | 1991 = 31 | 1992 = 32 | 1993 = 33 |
| 1994 = 34 | 1995 = 35 | 1996 = 36 | 1997 = 37 |
| 1998 = 38 | 1999 = 39 | **2000** = Date codes dropped, year of production added after S/N. Production Series dropped to one letter, S/N moved from 4 digits to 6 digits to 9 digits with leading zeros used as placeholders. | |

\* = Limited or interrupted production years.

**A-4 Bulgarian Production Codes**

Some Late 1999 Production models may be found with a "39" S/N code and the Year 2000 after the S/N. These are pistols that were assembled from parts and frames that were made in 1999. Some Makarov pistols made for commercial export are also stamped with year of production, or non-standard S/N series at the request of the Importer. (Example, Miltex Commercial and Special Edition series and "Arsenal Brand" export models)

Example:
Old Style numbering system AB 21 1441 = 1981 production, 1441 unit in the "AB" series.

New Style numbering system A001441 2001 (full year given, no Dash used) or A001441 - 01 (last two digits of year used, dash between S/N and Year).

It is possible to have two pistols with the same unit number but a different series number under the Old Style Numbering system.

Example:
AB 19 1441 and KO 19 1441 are two different pistols. This is what lead to the X'ing out of non-English letters in the S/N, or in some cases a new S/N being issued to a pistol for importation to the US if the modified S/N was already of file with USA BATF, or the resulting number did not conform to guidelines.

*Bulgarian date code information compiled from information from Patman, ScottB, M. Madden (www.makarovinfo.com) and SlimTim from the Makarov.com /*

*Gunboards.com Makarov Forum and Mr. "O" of the "Arsenal" Factory (name with held at his request). Copyright Makarov.com, LLC, 2002, Hurricane, WV.*

## Germany (post-unification)

As early as the 1960s, the Russian Makarov pistol design was licensed to other socialist states, including East Germany. After the German reunification, the German Bundeswehr and republic came into possession of not only Makarov pistols, but the manufacturing site of Ernst Thaelmann in Suhl (state of Thueringen).

After some negotiations, the site became the Suhler Jagd- und Sportwaffen GmBH (Suhl Hunting and Sport Arms Ltd). The site included a substantial amount of manufacturing equipment, spare parts, drawings, and highly skilled personnel.

In 1994, the idea was spawned to once again make Makarov pistols from the existing stock of parts. One of the design features that were criticized was a cam that held the hammer in place (forward) when the safety was on "safe." This was removed on the new pistols such that the slide can now be racked when the pistols is on "safe," clearing the chamber if a round is present.

Several prototypes with various finishes and serial numbers V000001 to V000005 were made and V000006 through V000016 received a black finish. "V" is from Versuchsserie (trial series). One pistol was also made in 9mm Kurz (.380 ACP).

In 1995 then production of the mini-series starting with serial # 000001 began. The left of the slide was marked "SIMSON SUHL/THUR" (with Umlaut - the two dots - on the "U" in "THUR") and the right is marked with a blacksmith symbol and "MAKAROV 9x18mm". There appears to be some variation on this, since the pistols with serial numbers in the mid-400s and the ones in the 700s only say "SIMSON SUHL" without the "THUR." Considering that the original production run was only scheduled to yield approximately 300 pistols and that serial numbers in the 700s are now being sold, it is conceivable that full-scale production has been resumed.

The pistols were shipped in either a black or blue plastic box with manual and 2 new magazines that have the same raised area as the East German magazines. The manual gives the basic safety and operation of the pistol and a short paragraph on the history. The finish is black and the grips are a hard plastic with thumb rest and fine stippling on the sides and above the thumb rest.

The ones that found their way into the US are also marked with the importer's mark of "C.D.I. Swan. VT." The pistols were sold for a brief period during October-November 1997 by SOG.

# Appendix B - Holsters

There are various manufacturers offering better options than the issued leather Makarov holster. Fobus, Bladetech, Survival Sheath, and Uncle Mike's all make quality holsters for the PM and PMM Makarov pistols.

**Figure B-1 Fobus paddle holster for Makarov (VSS-MAK1)**

Fobus Paddle Holster for Makarov (VSS-MAK1 or roto (rotating the angle) model of VSS-MAK1RP)

**Figure B-2 Fobus roto paddle accessories for Makarov**

The Fobus roto model can be configured to fit the roto shoulder holster harness (VSS-SHR2), the universal vehicle/home mount (VSS-UVM), and the drop leg thigh harness (VSS-FOB-TTR). Glock pistol shown in photos.

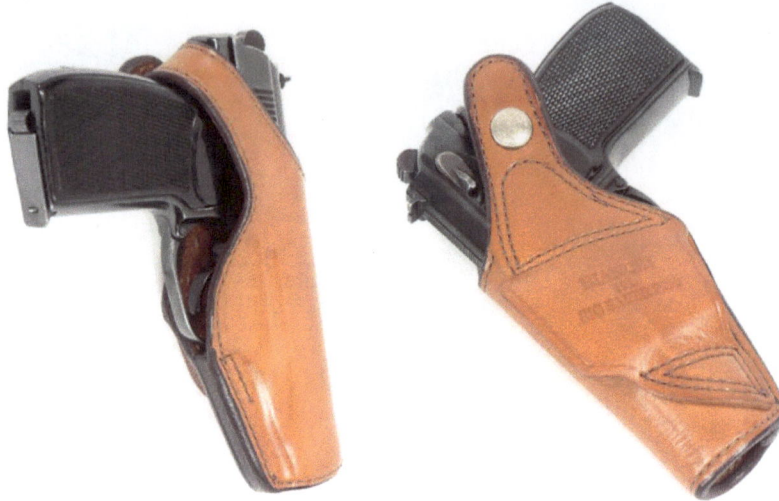

**Figure B-3 Bianchi Belt Holster for Makarov (VSS-BIA10704)**

Offering an initial tight fit but once broken in, this holster is a very good daily carry type holster that is comfortable and retained with the thumb break.

# Appendix C - Ammunition

9 x 18 mm Makarov is manufactured by many different countries and some can be rather old. Ensure you have 9 x 18mm Makarov ammunition; this ammunition is easily confused for 9 x 19mm NATO (9mm Luger) and .380 Automatic. Inspect it for uniformity, cleanliness, and serviceability. Check all for un-dented primers and only use issued ammunition. Many US manufacturers are making very high-quality 9 x 18 ammunition with modern bullets for self defense.

**Figure C-1**

**Figure C-2 Russian 95 grain, FMJ, 1033 feet per second**

**Figure C-3 Hornady 95 grain, JHP, 1000 feet per second**

# Appendix D - Ammunition Comparison

| 9x18mm Makarov | 9x19mm Luger | 7.62x25mm Tokarev | .45 ACP |
| --- | --- | --- | --- |

**PISTOLS AND SUBMACHINE GUNS**

## Size Comparison of NATO vs. Non-Standard Ammunition

| 5.56x 45mm | 5.45x 39mm | 5.56x 45mm | 7.62x 39mm | 7.62x 51mm | 7.62x 54R mm | 12.7x 99mm | 12.7x 108mm |
| --- | --- | --- | --- | --- | --- | --- | --- |

**ASSAULT RIFLES**          **SNIPER RIFLES & MACHINE GUNS**

# Appendix E - Non-Standard Ammunition Packaging & Markings

## Packaging

Russian small arms cartridges are packed in sealed sheet-metal containers, with two containers per wooden crate. Older Russian production used rectangular containers of heavy gauge galvanized iron with soldered seams. Around 1959, the introduction of painted, rolled edge, rounded corner, tin plate 'sardine can' containers became the standard.

Metal and wooden crates have standardized markings that identify the contents as to caliber, functional type, cartridge case material, quantity and cartridge/powder lot data. Specialized cartridges are further identified by a color code consisting of one or two color stripes which correspond to bullet tip color. AP cartridges with tungsten carbide cores are identified by two concentric circles instead of color stripes. Russian cartridge designation, packaging and marking practices are generally followed by former Soviet-Bloc countries; each, however, has introduced some modifications in designation and marking. Russian ammunition packaging can be distinguished from Bulgarian packaging, which also carries Cyrillic markings, primarily by the different factory codes. The factory code on the container also appears in the headstamp of the cartridges in the container.

**Steel Ammo Tins**
(Sardine Cans)

**Wood Ammo Crate (Case)**
(Contains 2 Tins + Opener)

**Cartridge quantities and weights of wooden crates**

| Country | Manufacturer | Caliber | Rounds /Crate | Crate Weight |
|---|---|---|---|---|
| Czech Rep. | Sellier and Bellot | 14.5 x 114 | 210 | 53 kg. |
| India | OFB | 14.5 x 114 | 60 | 15.5 kg. |
| Russia | Unknown | 14.5 x 114 | 80 | 23 kg. |
| Bulgaria | Arsenal | 12.7 x 108 | 200 | 29 kg. |
| Bulgaria | Arsenal | 12.7 x 108 | 200 | 32 kg. |
| Pakistan | POF | 12.7 x 108 | 280 | 42 kg. |
| Russia | Unknown | 12.7 x 108 | 190 | 29 kg. |
| Russia | Novosibirsk | 12.7 x 108 | 160 | 25 kg. |
| Bulgaria | Arsenal | 7.62 x 54(R) | 880 | 25 kg. |
| Czech Rep. | Sellier and Bellot | 7.62 x 54(R) | 800 | 24 kg. |
| Russia | Novosibirsk | 7.62 x 54(R) | 880 | 26 kg. |
| Russia | Novosibirsk | 7.62 x 54(R) | 600 | 21 kg. |
| Russia | Unknown | 7.62 x 54(R) | 880 | 26 kg. |
| Serbia | Prvi Partizan | 7.62 x 54(R) | 1,200 | 39 kg. |
| Czech Rep. | Sellier and Bellot | 7.62 x 39 | 1,200 | 28 kg. |
| Pakistan | POF | 7.62 x 39 | 1,750 | 39 kg. |
| Russia | Barnaul | 7.62 x 39 | 1,320 | 30 kg. |
| Serbia | Prvi Partizan | 7.62 x 39 | 1,260 | 29 kg. |
| Sudan | STC | 7.62 x 39 | 1,500 | 28.1 kg. |
| Ukraine | Lugansk | 7.62 x 39 | 1,320 | 30 kg. |
| Yugoslavia | Igman Zavod | 7.62 x 39 | 1,260 | 28 kg. |
| Yugoslavia | Igman Zavod | 7.62 x 39 | 1,120 | 27.5 kg. |
| Russia | Unknown | 5.45 x 39 | 2,160 | 29 kg. |
| Ukraine | Lugansk | 5.45 x 39 | 2,160 | 29 kg. |

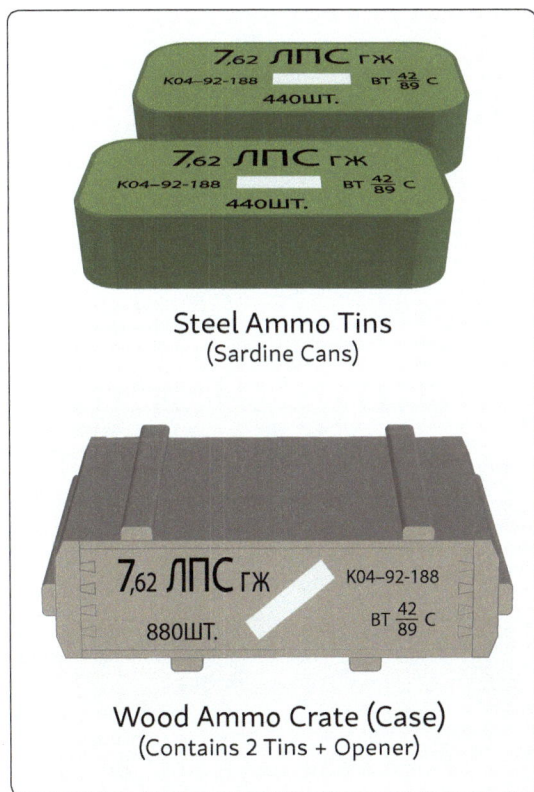

## Non-Standard Ammunition tin and crate marking - diagrams

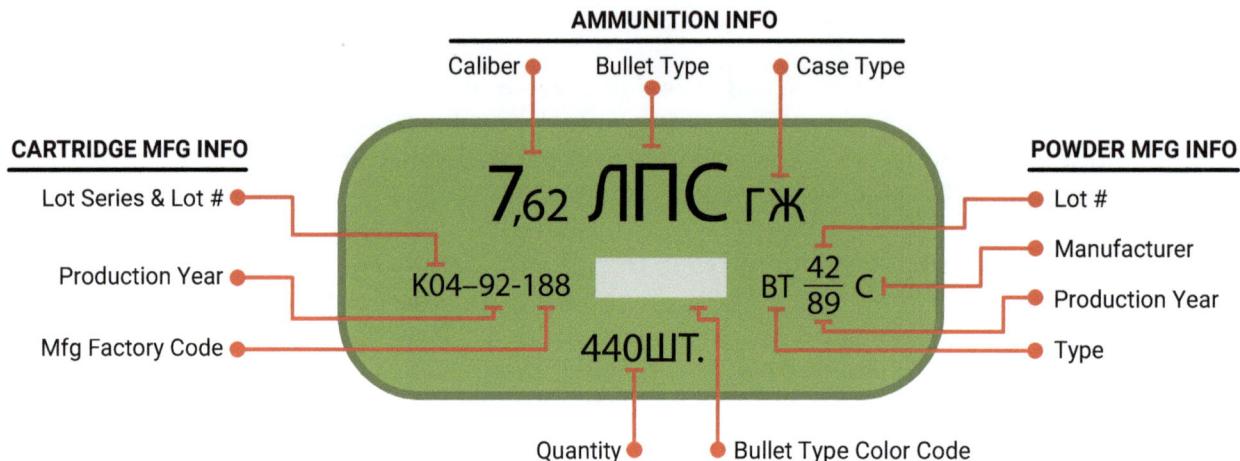

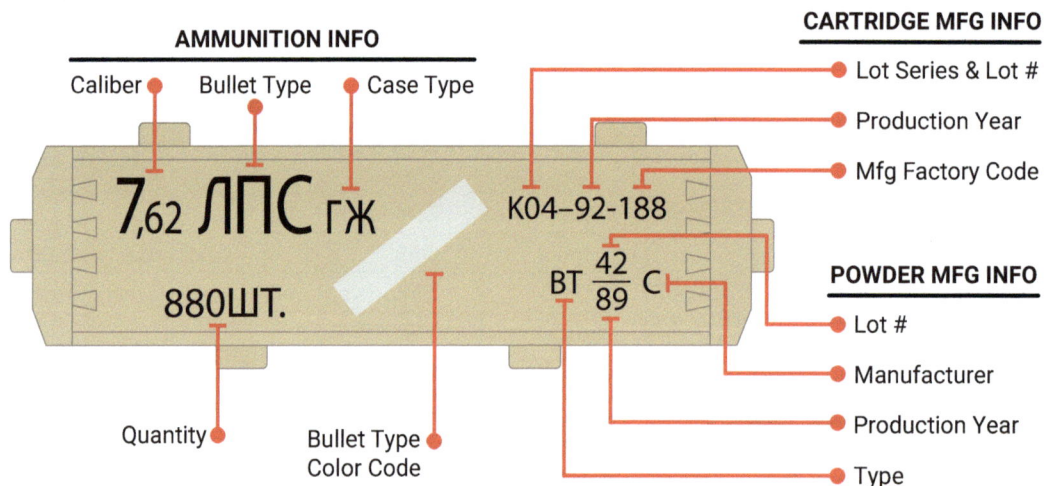

**AMMUNITION INFO**

Caliber • | Bullet Type • | Case Type •

**CARTRIDGE MFG INFO**

Lot Series & Lot # •

Production Year •

Mfg Factory Code •

# 7,62 ЛПС ГЖ

K04–92-188

440ШТ.

BT $\frac{42}{89}$ C

**POWDER MFG INFO**

• Lot #

• Manufacturer

• Production Year

• Type

Quantity • | • Bullet Type Color Code

---

**AMMUNITION INFO**

Caliber • | Bullet Type • | Case Type •

**CARTRIDGE MFG INFO**

• Lot Series & Lot #

• Production Year

• Mfg Factory Code

# 7,62 ЛПС ГЖ

880ШТ.

K04–92-188

BT $\frac{42}{89}$ C

**POWDER MFG INFO**

• Lot #

• Manufacturer

• Production Year

• Type

Quantity • | Bullet Type Color Code •

## Non-Standard Ammunition tin and crate marking - Russian ammunition data

### CASE TYPE MARKINGS

| Mark | Meaning |
|------|---------|
| ГЖ | Bimetallic case (gilding metal clad steel) |
| ГЛ | Brass case |
| ГС | Steel case |

### CARTRIDGE MFG FACTORY CODES

| Code | Location |
|------|----------|
| 3 | Ulyanovsk |
| 17 | Barnaul |
| 38 | Yuryuzan |
| 60 | Frunze (now Bishkek) |
| 188 | Novosibirsk |
| 270 | Voroshilovgrad (now Luhansk) |
| 304 | Lugansk |
| 539 | Tula |
| 711 | Klimovsk |
| T | Tula |

# Non-Standard Ammunition tin and crate marking - Russian ammunition data

## BULLET TYPE MARKINGS

| Mark | Meaning |
|---|---|
| Б<br>Б-30<br>Б-32<br>БП | Armor-piercing |
| БЗ | Armor-piercing incendiary |
| БЗТ<br>БЗТ-44 | Armor-piercing incendiary tracer |
| БС<br>БС-40<br>БС-41 | Armor-piercing with special core of tungsten carbide instead of carbon steel |
| БСТ | Armor-piercing with tungsten carbide core with added tracer |
| БТ | Armor-piercing tracer |
| Д | Heavy (long-range) with lead core instead of carbon steel |
| З<br>ЗП | Incendiary |
| Л | Lightweight bullet |
| ЛПС | Light ball bullet with mild steel core |
| МДЗ | High explosive incendiary |
| П<br>П-41 | Spotting / ranging |
| ПЗ | Incendiary spotting / ranging |
| ПП | Enhanced penetration |
| ПС | Spotting / ranging with mild steel core |
| ПТ | Spotting / ranging tracer |
| СНБ | Armor-piercing sniper |
| Т<br>Т-30<br>Т-45<br>Т-46 | Tracer |
| 57-У-322<br>57-У-323 | Cartridge with higher powder charge |
| 57-У-423 | High-pressure cartridge |
| 57-Х-322<br>57-Х-323<br>57-Х-340 | Blank cartridge |
| 57-НЕ-УЧ | Training cartridge |
| 7Н1 | Sniper bullet |

## BULLET TYPE COLOR CODES (Ammunition up to 14.5mm)

| Color | Meaning |
|---|---|
| No color | Ball |
| White tip | Reference Ball |
| Silver tip | Light ball with steel core |
| Yellow tip | Heavy ball, or ball with torpedo base (on 7.62x54R) |
| Blue tip + white band | Short range ball 14.5x114 (only Hungarian and Czech) |
| Green tip + white band | Short range, tracer, (only Czech designation, only found on 7.62x39 with round nose) |
| Green tip | Tracer |
| Green tip & head-stamp or entire cartridge green | Subsonic ammunition for silencer-weapons |
| Red tip | Spotting charge, incendiary |
| Red tip + white band | Short range tracer ball 14.5x114 (only Hungarian designation) |
| Entire bullet red | High explosive bullet (7.62x54R after 1945) |
| Entire bullet red | High explosive bullet (on 12.7 and 14.5mm) |
| Magenta tip + red band | Armor piercing incendiary tracer |
| Black tip + red band | Armor piercing incendiary |
| Black tip + red shell | Armor piercing incendiary with tungsten carbide core |
| Black tip + yellow band | Armor piercing incendiary Phosphorus 12.7 |
| Black tip | Armor piercing |

** The bullet tip color codes in the table above will be the same color codes on the tins or crates, but they will be color stripes on the packaging.

*Example:*

CARTRIDGE
Black Tip + Red Band

TIN or CRATE
Black Stripe + Red Stripe

# Appendix F - Non-Standard Weapon Identification Markings

## General Identification Markings

There are various identification markings found on non-standard weapons. Typically the markings will provide some or all of the following information:
- factory name or stamp (proof mark)
- caliber & serial number
- selector lever markings/symbols
- rear sight mark/symbol

### Selector Lever Markings on Kalashnikov Rifles

| Upper/ Safe Symbol | Mid/ Full-Auto Symbol | Lower/ Semi-Auto Symbol | Country |
|---|---|---|---|
| | Д | 1 | Albania |
| | L | D | Albania |
| | АВ | ЕД | Bulgaria |
| | L | D | China |
| | 进 | 单 | China |
| | 30 | 1 | Czechoslovakia |
| | آلی | خرد | Egypt |
| | D | E | Egypt |
| | D | E | East Germany |
| | ∞ | 1 | Hungary |
| أ | ص | م | Iraq |
| | 련 | 단 | North Korea |
| | C | P | Poland |
| | Z | O | Poland |
| S | A | R | Romania |
| S | FA | FF | Romania |
| | 1 | 3 | Romania |
| | ЛР | ОГОНЬ | Russia |
| | АВ | ОД | Russia |
| U | R | Ɔ | Yugo/Serbia |

### Rear Sight Marks on Kalashnikov Rifles

| Symbol | Country |
|---|---|
| D | Albania |
| П | Bulgaria |
| D | China |
| N | East Germany |
| A | Hungary |
| 口 | North Korea |
| S | Poland |
| P | Romania |
| П | Russia |
| O | Yugo/Serbia |

*NOTE: Data tables are not all inclusive, but they cover the more common weapon manufacturers.*

# Non-Standard Weapon Identification Markings

## Factory Stamps and Countries of Manufacture

The table of symbols below are factory stamps (proof marks) for non-standard weapons. The symbols will identify the country of manufacture of the weapon. NOTE: This is not an all inclusive list, but it covers the more common weapon manufacturers.

| | | | |
|---|---|---|---|
| (10) Bulgaria | (21) Bulgaria | (25) Bulgaria | China |
| (386) China | (36) China | (66) China | China |
| Egypt | East Germany | (3) East Germany | (K3) East Germany |
| East Germany | (06) East Germany | Iraq | Iraq |
| North Korea | North Korea | (11) Poland | Romania |
| Russia | Russia | Russia | Russia |
| Russia | Russia | Russia | Russia |
| Yugoslavia/Serbia | M.70.AB2 Yugoslavia/Serbia | ZASTAVA-KRAGUJEVAC Yugoslavia/Serbia | |

# Appendix G - Non-standard weapons theory overview

There are three key concepts to understand when manipulating non-standard weapons. These simple and logical concepts are:

1. CYCLE OF OPERATIONS
2. OPERATING SYSTEMS
3. LOCKING SYSTEMS

> Firearm design trends are shared across region, manufacturer and class of weapon and are relatively obvious to recognize.
>
> Keep in mind that firearms are essentially simple machines that harness the energy created by the fired cartridge to operate the system.

### CYCLE OF OPERATIONS (COO)

The cycle of operations is a crucial basis for understanding how the weapon operates and for function/malfunction diagnosis. Each specific malfunction will correspond to a specific step or sometimes two in the COO. A failure in the system at a certain point, will by default, cause a failure of omission of all subsequent steps. (example – a failure to properly extract will manifest as a failure to eject.)

The COO will vary based on the type of operating and locking systems. Once the operating and locking systems of the weapon are known, the COO is logical.

*The examples below all start from a standard reference point: the weapon is loaded, charged, placed on fire and the trigger is pulled.*

## 'Cycle of Operations' Examples:

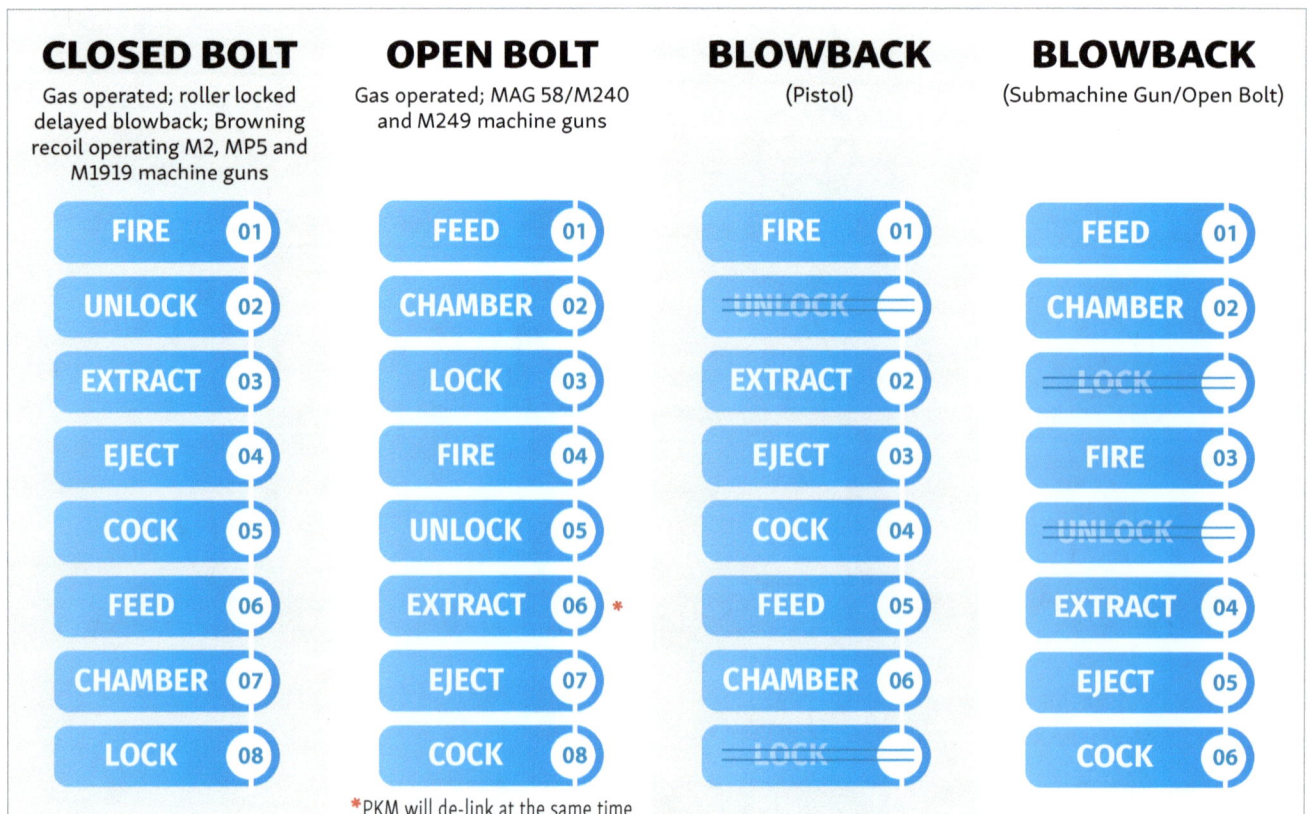

| CLOSED BOLT | OPEN BOLT | BLOWBACK | BLOWBACK |
|---|---|---|---|
| Gas operated; roller locked delayed blowback; Browning recoil operating M2, MP5 and M1919 machine guns | Gas operated; MAG 58/M240 and M249 machine guns | (Pistol) | (Submachine Gun/Open Bolt) |
| FIRE 01 | FEED 01 | FIRE 01 | FEED 01 |
| UNLOCK 02 | CHAMBER 02 | ~~UNLOCK~~ | CHAMBER 02 |
| EXTRACT 03 | LOCK 03 | EXTRACT 02 | ~~LOCK~~ |
| EJECT 04 | FIRE 04 | EJECT 03 | FIRE 03 |
| COCK 05 | UNLOCK 05 | COCK 04 | ~~UNLOCK~~ |
| FEED 06 | EXTRACT 06 * | FEED 05 | EXTRACT 04 |
| CHAMBER 07 | EJECT 07 | CHAMBER 06 | EJECT 05 |
| LOCK 08 | COCK 08 | ~~LOCK~~ | COCK 06 |

*PKM will de-link at the same time

# Non-standard weapons theory overview *(continued ...)*

## ⚙ OPERATING SYSTEMS

1. **Direct Impingement**- a type of gas operation that directs gas from a fired cartridge directly to the bolt carrier or slide assembly to cycle the action. (AR-15/M4 variants)

2. **Long-stroke piston system**- the piston is mechanically fixed to the bolt group and moves through the entire operating cycle. (AK variants)

3. **Short-stroke piston system (tappet system)**- the piston moves separately from the bolt group. It may directly push the bolt group parts as n the M1 carbine or operate through a connecting rod. (HK 416, AR180, POF, LWRC, FN FAL)

4. **Blowback**- the system of operation for self-loading firearms that obtains energy from the motion of the cartridge case as it is pushed to the rear by expanding gases created by the ignition of the propellant charge. (STEN, Makarov, M3 Grease Gun)

5. **Short recoil action**- the barrel and slide recoil only a short distance before they unlock and separate. The barrel stops quickly, and the slide continues rearward compressing the recoil spring and performing extraction, ejection and finally feeding a fresh round from the magazine in the counter recoil phase. During the last portion of its forward travel, the slide locks into the barrel and pushes the barrel back into battery. *(This is found in most handguns chambered for 9x19mm Parabellum or greater caliber. Smaller calibers, 9x18mm Makarov and below, generally use the blowback method of operation due to lower chamber pressure and associated simplicity of design.)

6. **Roller-locked, delayed-blowback**- when the bolt is closed, the rollers carried in the bolt are wedged into the receiver recesses. On firing, the rollers must be forced out of the recesses at great mechanical disadvantage, delaying the opening of the bolt, even with full power 7.62mm NATO (.308 Winchester) rifle cartridges used in the G3/HK 91 (G3, HK 91, HK 93, HK 53, MP5 variants)

7. **Inertia operated systems**- the bolt body is separated from the locked bolt body to remain stationary while the recoiling gun and locked bolt head moves rearward. This movement compresses the spring between the bolt head and bolt body, storing the energy required to cycle the action. Benelli shotguns.

# Non-standard weapons theory overview *(continued ...)*

## 🔒 LOCKING SYSTEMS

1. **None** - all blowback pistols and some submachine guns – (STEN, UZI, M3 Grease Gun, Makarov, and CZ 82)

2. **Roller** - (HK variants, MG3, MG34, MG 42 and CZ 52)

3. **Rotating bolt** - (AK, Stoner, M60, and M249)

4. **Tilting bolt** - (SKS, FN FAL and MAG 58/M240)

5. **Tilting barrel** - (Tokarev TT33, Sig variants, M1911 variants and Glock variants)

6. **Rotating barrel** - (MAB P15, Colt All American 2000, and Beretta 8000)

7. **Locking flaps** - (RPD, DP/DPM and DShK)

8. **Falling locking block** - (P38, M9, and VZ58)

## Function check
Checking the mechanical function of a weapon by replicating, without ammunition, the firing modes from the lowest rate of fire (SAFE if applicable) to the highest in a progressive sequence (not by selector location). The parts checked are the safety/safeties, sear and disconnector.

### M4A1
1. Ensure the rifle is clear
2. Charge and place the weapon on SAFE
3. Attempt to fire (weapons should not FIRE, safety is functioning)
4. Place the weapon on SEMI, pull the trigger and hold it to the rear (hammer should fall, trigger/sear functioning)
5. Maintain the trigger to the rear and cycle the bolt
6. Release the trigger and listen for a metallic click (disconnector functioning)
7. Pull the trigger again and the hammer should fall
8. Charge the weapon and place on AUTO
9. Pull the trigger and hold it to the rear then cycle the bolt more than once
10. Release the trigger and pull it again, nothing should happen (auto sear is functioning)
11. Charge the weapon then pull the trigger again and the hammer should fall
12. Function check complete

## Significant visual indicators
- Any checked, knurled or serrated surface
- Any movable lever or switch
- Pins with gripping surfaces
- Index marks (two lines that need to be aligned to disassembled (CZ 75)
- Recoil spring with ends of different diameters

www.ingramcontent.com/pod-product-compliance
Lightning Source LLC
Chambersburg PA
CBHW061056090426
42742CB00002B/63